Timeline of Slavery

MW00717449

Yosef is sold as a slave
Age 17

G-d tells Avraham:
Your children will be strangers in a land that is not theirs.
They will be slaves for 400 years.
Afterwards, they will leave with great wealth.
Then they will return to this land (Israel) which I have given them.

Yosef becomes the ruler in Egypt
He begins to store food in preparation for the seven years of hunger
Age 30

13 years later

9 years later

Yosef passes away
Age 110

There is a famine in Egypt and in Israel
Yosef invites his father, Yaakov, and his family (70 people) to move from Israel to Egypt

23 years later

71 years later

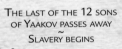

The last of the 12 sons of Yaakov passes away
~ Slavery begins ~

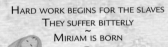

Hard work begins for the slaves
They suffer bitterly
Miriam is born

Aharon is born

3 years later

Moshe is born

30 years later

3 years later

79 years later

The Ten Plagues begin

The Jews leave Egypt

EXIT

1 year later

The 400 Years

The 400 years of enslavement is counted from the birth of Yitzchak until the Exodus.
The Jews lived in Egypt for 210 years.
They were slaves to Pharaoh for 116 of those years.
They suffered the last 86 years from the harsh labor.

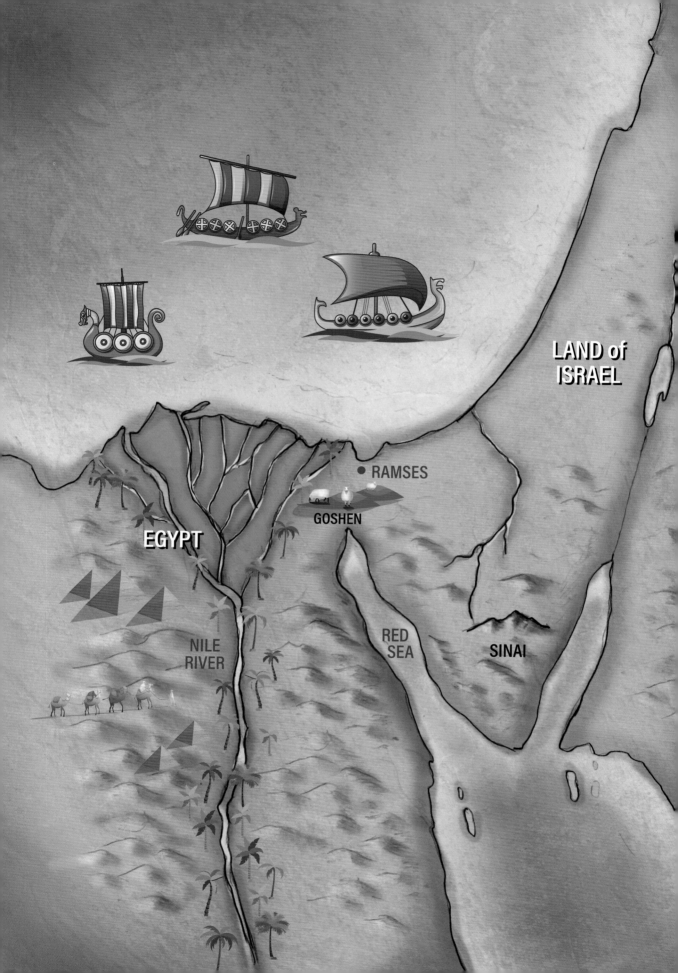

LAND of ISRAEL

RAMSES

GOSHEN

EGYPT

NILE RIVER

RED SEA

SINAI

The Passover Book
From Slavery to Freedom

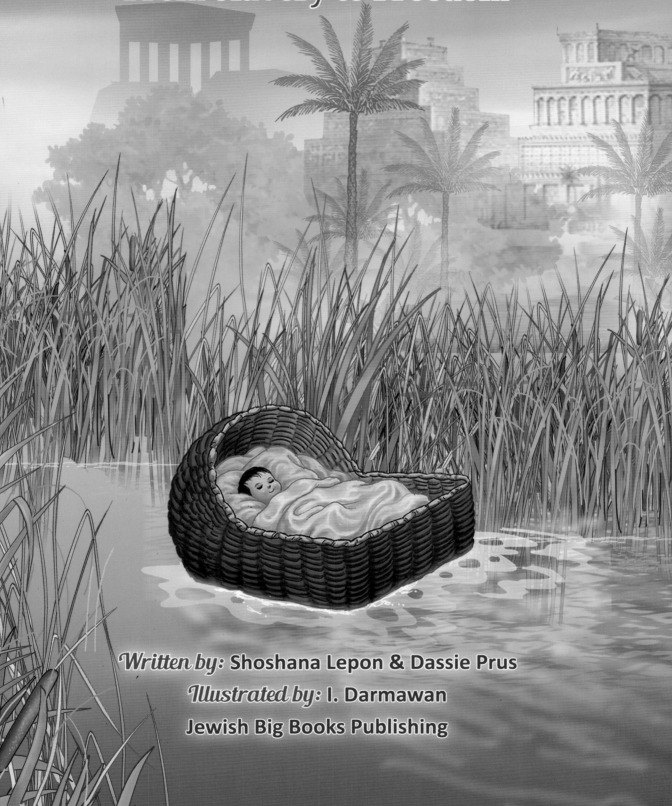

Written by: Shoshana Lepon & Dassie Prus

Illustrated by: I. Darmawan

Jewish Big Books Publishing

Long, long ago, when our nation began,
we were slaves to Pharaoh, in Egypt, his land.
We had to make bricks to build up his city.
It was hot, dirty work and the king had no pity.

1

Women and men had to work hard and long,
without any rest, and that was so wrong.
And we would still be there, to this very day,
if G-d had not sent Moshe our way.

The magicians of Egypt read the stars and the moon.
They said a boy would be born someday soon
who would grow up and come to free all the Jews!
Pharaoh was filled with great fear at this news.

Pharaoh called in the Jewish nurses to say:
"Don't let the baby boys live, starting today!"
The nurses were Miriam and Yocheved, her mother,
who feared G-d much more than they feared any other.

They knew G-d was putting them both to the test.
Could they stand up to Pharaoh? They'd sure try their best
They cared for the babies, tucked them safely in bed,
making sure they were happy and warm and well-fed.

Their neighbors, the Egyptians, sneaked over and spied
to report newborn babies the Jews tried to hide.
Yocheved and Amram hid their new son away
until he got bigger and could no longer stay.

Yocheved took reeds and tar to build him a boat
and in the Nile River she put him to float.

7

Big sister Miriam stood guard on the shore,
never imagining what was in store.
Pharaoh's daughter came down to bathe in the Nile,
with maids from the palace to serve her in style.

Was that a small boat, floating there, downstream?
She stretched out her arm, as if in a dream.
"It's a Jewish baby. He's crying, poor thing!
Were they trying to save him from my father, the king?"

She named the child Moshe and passed him around,
but her maids could not get him to drink and calm down.
Suddenly Miriam stepped up to suggest,
"Maybe a Jewish nurse would be the best?"

She knew just the one who could feed her brother.
She ran and brought back his very own mother.

Moshe lived like a prince in the home of the king;
as the grandson of Pharaoh he could have anything.

Yet Moshe the prince felt the pain of the slave,
helping his brothers, showing how to be brave.
Pharaoh grew angry at his caring and kindness
so Moshe had to run from his Royal Highness.

12

One day in the desert where the sand meets the skies,
Moshe saw a great wonder in front of his eyes.
A bush was on fire; its leaves filled with flame.
Yet it didn't burn up. It remained just the same.

From inside the fire, he heard G-d's command:
"Go lead My people from Egypt's land."
Moshe asked, "Who am I to be chosen to go?
My speech is not clear, my words come out slow."

G-d said, "Who made your mouth able to talk?
Who gave you the power to hear, see and walk?
It is I! I will help you with every word
and Aharon, your brother, will make sure that you're heard."

14

Moshe and Aharon came with G-d's command:
"Let My people go! Let them leave Egypt's land!"
Pharaoh laughed out loud. "Who orders me so?
I am the king. My slaves shall not go!"

But Pharaoh just laughed.
"That's the best you can do?"
So G-d sent out frogs
in Plague Number Two.

Still the king did not bend
so stubborn was he.
Itchy lice crawled all over
in Plague Number Three.

Wild beasts came next,
breaking down every door.
Lions, tigers and bears
in Plague Number Four.

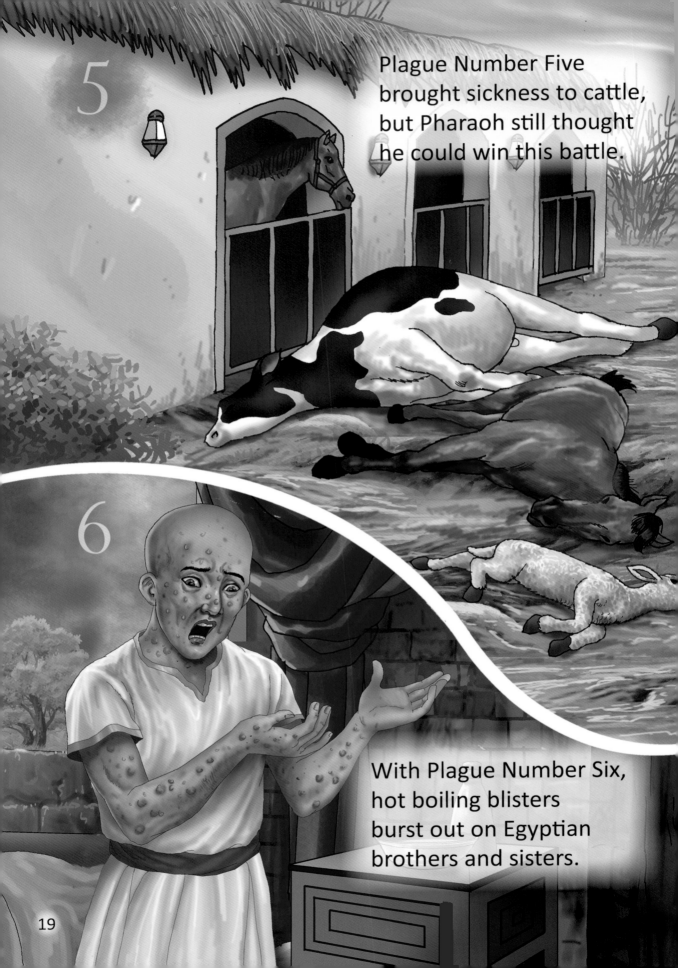

5 Plague Number Five brought sickness to cattle, but Pharaoh still thought he could win this battle.

6 With Plague Number Six, hot boiling blisters burst out on Egyptian brothers and sisters.

Now it was time
for Plague Number Seven.
Fiery hailstones
rained down from heaven.

7

8

Swarms of locusts attacked
in Plague Number Eight.
They chewed up the trees;
the destruction was great.

During Plague Number Nine it was darker than night
and none of the Egyptians could move left or right.
But the Jews could see what was hidden away
buried in chests and in jugs made of clay.

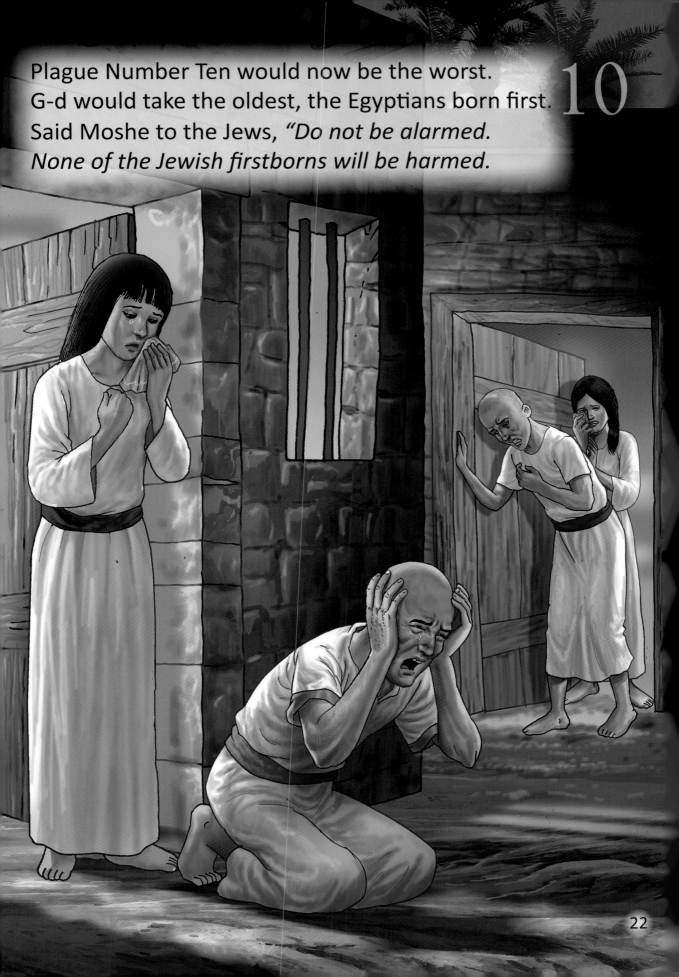

Plague Number Ten would now be the worst.
G-d would take the oldest, the Egyptians born first.
Said Moshe to the Jews, *"Do not be alarmed.*
None of the Jewish firstborns will be harmed.

10

"Each family must take a young lamb to roast,
and paint with its blood upon their doorpost.
Then G-d will pass over each Jewish home,
and He will have mercy and save us, alone."

23

At midnight in Egypt the last plague took place,
and Pharaoh ran to Moshe with fear on his face.
He cried, *"You must leave now. Please don't wait!*
Go serve your G-d, His power is great!"

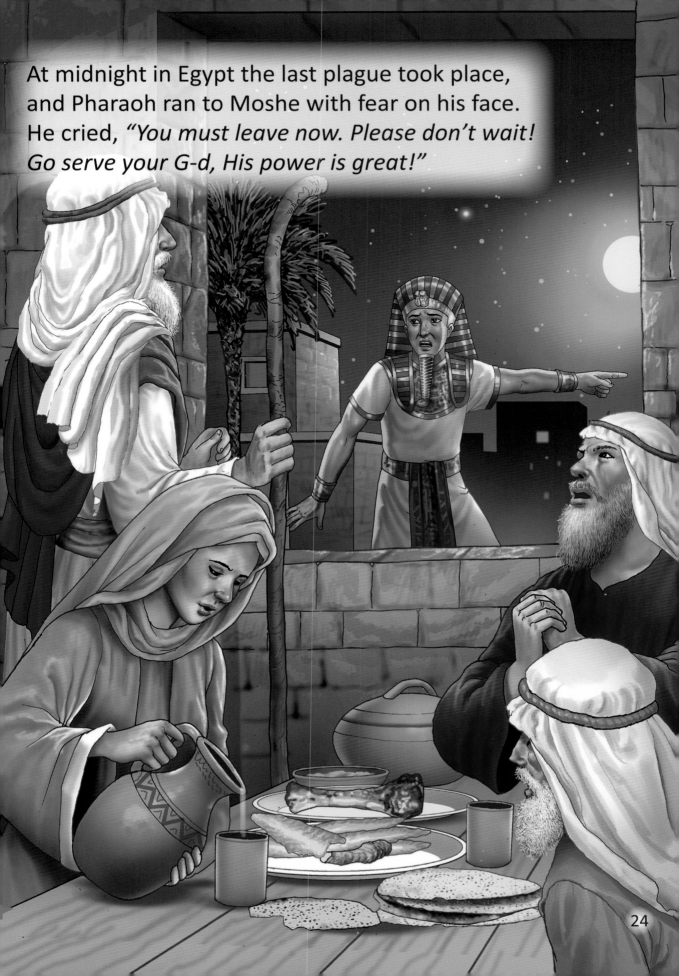

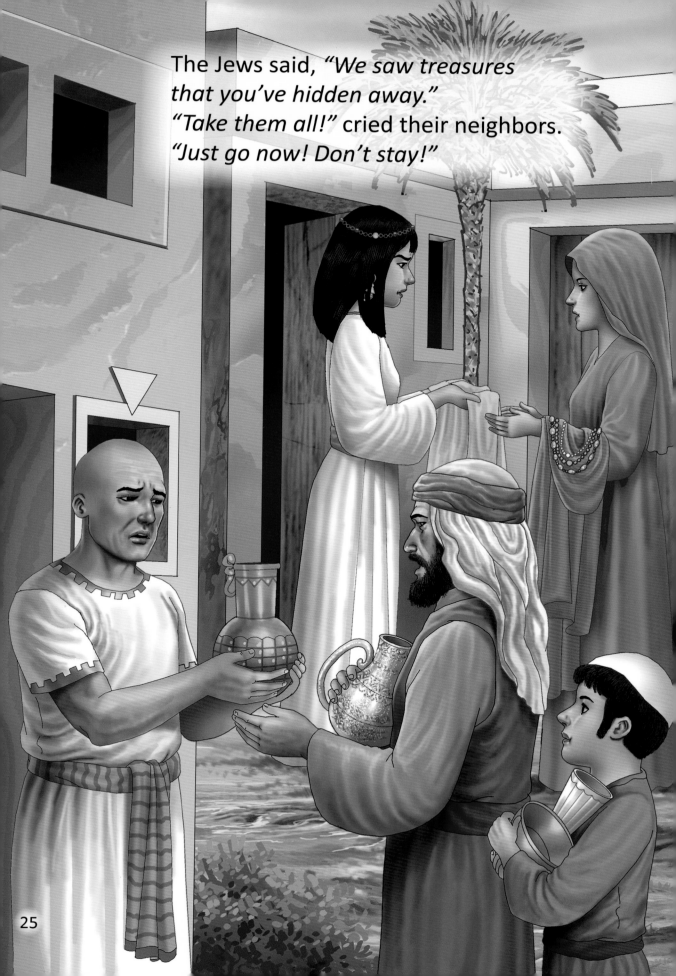

The Jews said, *"We saw treasures that you've hidden away."*
"Take them all!" cried their neighbors.
"Just go now! Don't stay!"

The Jews quickly filled up their sacks
and went out of Egypt with dough on their backs.
No time to let it rise; no time to let it bake.
They could only make thin matzah cake.

The Jews got to the sea with the waves rising high
and then from behind came a terrible cry.
Egypt's soldiers on horses had come to attack
because Pharaoh wanted his slaves to come back.

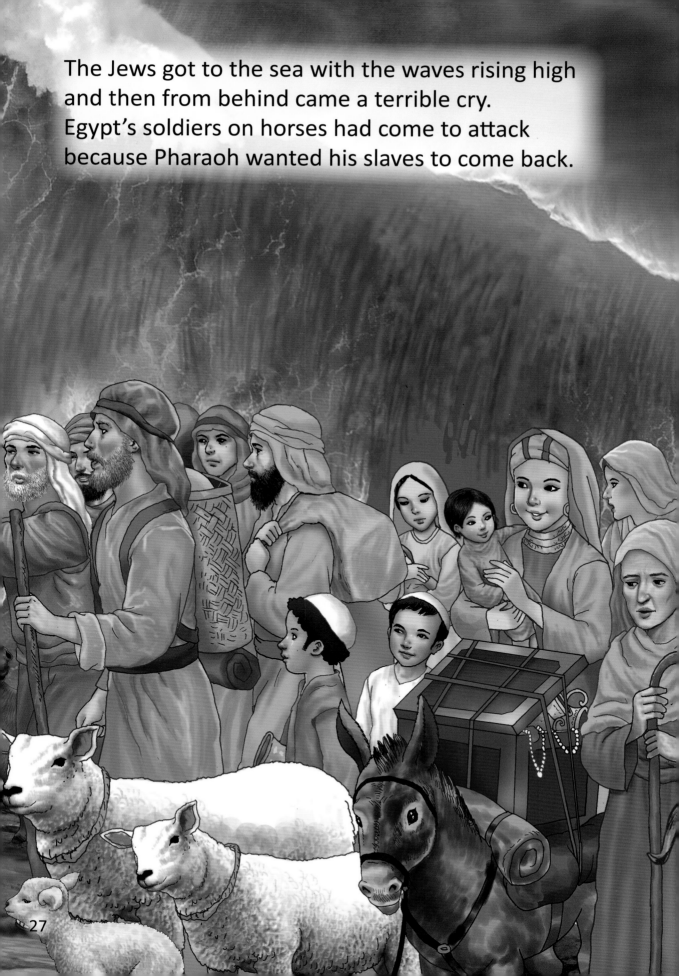

The Jews walked into the water despite their great fear
and the sea split for them, leaving land dry and clear.
Safely through the sea they passed on that day,
with G-d watching over them each step of the way.

The soldiers gave chase and charged into the dried up sea,
but the waves crashed back down, and our people were free!
Pharaoh really wanted all his slaves to stay,
but G-d freed us then, and we're still free today!

At the Passover Seder we tell all about
our slavery in Egypt and how G-d took us out.
We are free to be Jews and this is the sign:
matzah, maror and four cups of wine.

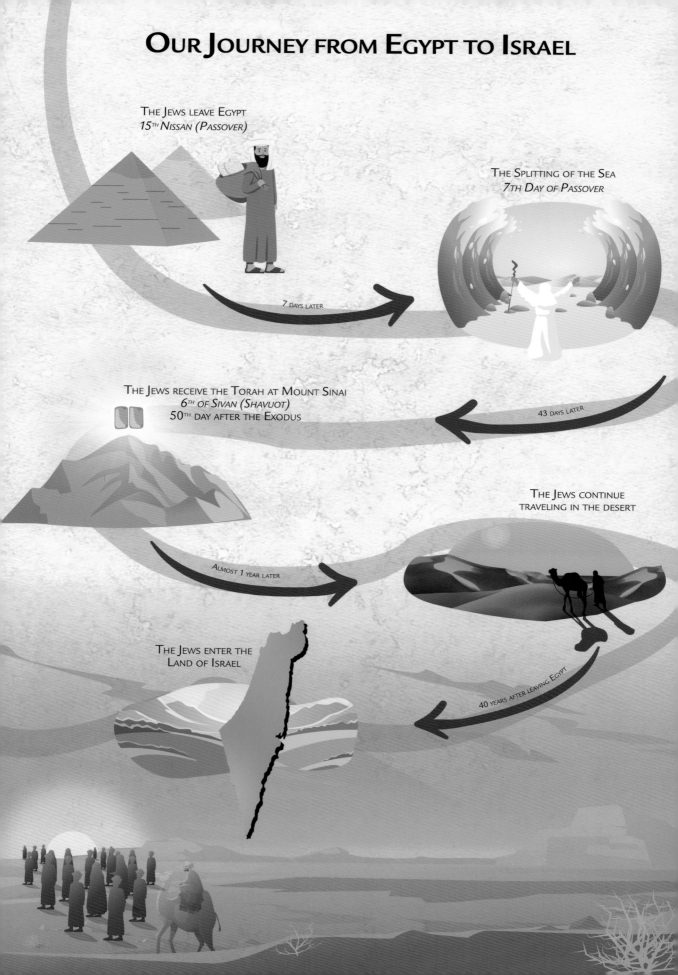

Our Journey from Egypt to Israel

The Jews leave Egypt
15th Nissan (Passover)

7 days later

The Splitting of the Sea
7th Day of Passover

43 days later

The Jews receive the Torah at Mount Sinai
6th of Sivan (Shavuot)
50th day after the Exodus

The Jews continue
traveling in the desert

Almost 1 year later

The Jews enter the
Land of Israel

40 years after leaving Egypt

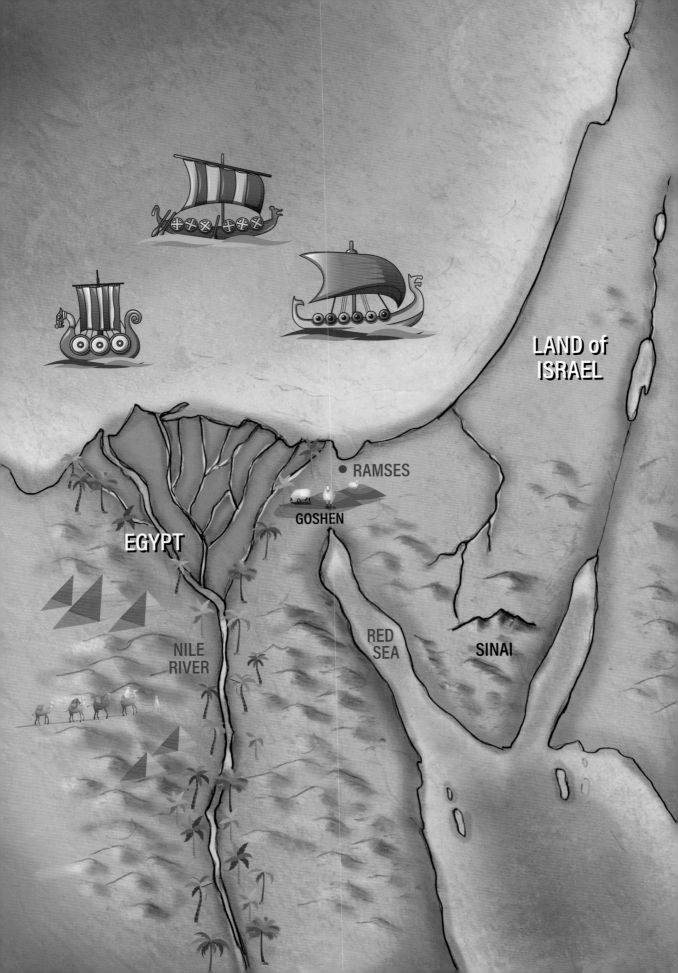

LAND of
ISRAEL

RAMSES

GOSHEN

EGYPT

NILE
RIVER

RED
SEA

SINAI

This book is dedicated to my dear father

Yaakov Baruch Gansburg of blessed memory,

who showed me how to live a life of faith, peace, generosity, and unwavering commitment to my values.

Sponsored by my dear mother,

Simone Gansburg,

who lovingly encourages and inspires me to pursue my dreams. - *D.P.*

To my dear children Levi, Miriam, Muleh, Zalman, Mussia, Yossi and Yisrael. - D.P.

In memory of my greatest fans, Carl & Pat Lepon, - S.L.

About the Authors

Shoshana Lepon is the author of many books for children and adults. She is also a shadchanit and real estate agent. She and her husband are blessed to live in Ramat Beit Shemesh with their children and grandchildren.

Dassie Prus co-directs the Chabad activities together with her husband and her seven children in Doylestown, PA. Aspiring to enhance the Jewish educational experience, she founded Jewish Big Books Publishing to create the exciting Jewish Big Book holiday series.

Glossary:

Aharon	Aaron
Maror	Bitter herbs such as horseradish and Romaine lettuce eaten at the Passover seder
Matzah	Unleavened flat bread eaten on Passover
Moshe	Moses
Seder	A ceremonial meal (with 15 steps) conducted on Passover celebrating the Exodus.

First Edition - 2020 / 5780
Second Edition - 2021 / 5781
Copyright © 2020 / 5780 Jewish Big Books Publishing
All rights reserved. No part of this publication may be reproduced, stored in a retrieval system or transmitted in any form or by any means without prior written permission of the publisher.
The Passover Book: From Slavery to Freedom
Authors: Shoshana Lepon & Dassie Prus
Illustrator: Iwan Darmawan
Family Tree and Maps: Dina Marer
SBN-13: 978-1-7325237-2-2
Jewish Big Books Publishing / www.JewishBigBooks.com
Printed in China
Printed by ShluchimServices.com / JewishInnovations.com

The characters depicted in this book are for illustrative purposes only. Their facial features are a creation of the illustrator.